GROUNDBREAKERS

Christopher Columbus

Struan Reid

Heinemann Library
Chicago, Illinois

© 2002 Reed Educational & Professional Publishing
Published by Heinemann Library,
an imprint of Reed Educational & Professional Publishing,
Chicago, Illinois

Customer Service 888-454-2279

Visit our website at www.heinemannlibrary.com

Designed by AMR
Illustrated by Art Construction
Originated by Ambassador Litho
Printed in China by Wing King Tong

06 05 04 03
10 9 8 7 6 5 4 3 2

Library of Congress Cataloging-in-Publication Data
Reid, Struan.
    Christopher Columbus / Struan Reid.
       p. cm. -- (Groundbreakers)
    Includes bibliographical references and index.
    Summary: Presents an account of Columbus's life and explorations and
    examines their impact on history and the world.
       ISBN 1-58810-593-8 (lib. bdg.)   ISBN 1-58810-986-0 (pbk. bdg.)
       1. Columbus, Christopher--Juvenile literature. 2.
    Explorers--America--Biography--Juvenile literature. 3.
    Explorers--Spain--Biography--Juvenile literature. 4. America--Discovery
    and exploration--Spanish--Juvenile literature. [1. Columbus,
    Christopher. 2. Explorers. 3. America--Discovery and
    exploration--Spanish.] I. Title. II. Series.
       E111 .R34 2002
       970.01'5'092--dc21

                                                                 2001004029

Acknowledgments
The publishers would like to thank the following for permission to reproduce photographs:
p. 4 Bridgeman/Metropolitan Museum of Art, New York; p. 5 Hereford Cathedral; pp. 6, 37
Mansell/Timepix; pp. 7, 12, 14, 17, 19, 20, 32 Mary Evans; pp. 8, 16 Woodfall Wild Images; p. 9
Bridgeman/Museu de Marinha, Lisbon; p. 10 Bridgeman/Prado, Madrid; pp. 11, 30 Colin Dixon;
p. 13 British Museum; pp. 15, 34, 39 Corbis; p. 18 Hulton Getty, p. 21 Robert Harding; pp. 22,
24 Travel Ink/Simon Reddy; p. 23 Michael Holford; p. 25 Bridgeman/Koninklijk Museum, Belgium;
p. 26 Travel Ink/David Toase; p. 27 Bridgeman; p. 29 National Maritime Museum; p. 33
Bridgeman/British Museum; p. 36 Travel Ink; p. 38 Bridgeman/Musee des Beaux-arts Andre
Malraux; p. 40 Dave Saunders; p. 41 Bridgeman/Royal Geographical Society.

Cover photograph reproduced with permission of Bridgeman.

Our thanks to Christopher Gibb for his comments in the preparation of this book.

Every effort has been made to contact copyright holders of any material reproduced in this
book. Any omissions will be rectified in subsequent printings if notice is given to the publishers.

Some words are shown in bold, **like this.** You can find out what
they mean by looking in the glossary.

Contents

The Shock of the New

People today can travel in airplanes from one side of the world to the other in less than a day. Our messages travel thousands of miles in seconds, bounced off satellites in the sky. We are surrounded with information about the countries of the world and their inhabitants.

Five hundred years ago, when Christopher Columbus lived, people had a completely different idea of the world. Most people traveled only very short distances to their nearest town, usually only on market days. Merchants and traders who traveled further afield told stories of mysterious foreign lands, but nobody knew much about them.

During the 15th century, this limited picture of the world began to change. Explorers were beginning to travel further and further away from their homelands. They were searching for a sea route to the East, where they hoped to find great riches— gold, silver, precious stones, and spices. Explorers returned with information about the lands they had found. Mapmakers could then draw more accurate maps of the world, with fewer blank spaces.

This is a map of the known world in the 15th century.

Inspiration

One of the greatest of these early explorers was Christopher Columbus. As a boy he had been inspired to sail to China, then known as Cathay, after reading the account of the travels of Marco Polo, a Venetian merchant, in the 13th century. In 1492, Columbus and his small crew set sail from Spain in three tiny ships, with no clear idea of where they were going or what they would find. What they did find at the end of their journey was an entire continent now called America. Although Vikings from Scandinavia had sailed there 500 years earlier, it had been long forgotten by Europeans. The lands Columbus "discovered" were rich, fertile, and ruled by astonishing civilizations.

True impact

Columbus never really understood the importance of his discovery. The New World eventually brought fabulous riches into Europe, but at a price. Europeans regarded these lands as theirs to **conquer** and plunder, and in so doing they destroyed ancient civilizations that had existed there for thousands of years.

In Columbus's words:

"Seven years passed in discussions [planning his expedition] and nine in the enterprise itself. Remarkable and memorable events took place in those years, which no one could have conceived beforehand."

(Taken from a letter written in 1500 by Columbus to the king and queen of Spain)

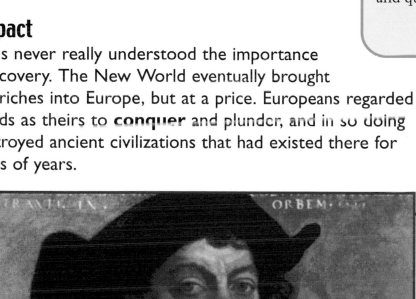

A portrait of Christopher Columbus by Italian artist Sebastiano del Piombo shows Columbus at the height of his fame, but it was painted in 1519, 13 years after his death.

Columbus's Early Life

Cristoforo (Christopher) Colombo was born in 1451 in the north Italian port of Genoa. He was the first child of Domenico, a wool weaver, and Susanna. Christopher was followed by two brothers named Bartolomeo and Diego, and a sister, Bianchinetta. Another brother, Giovanni, died very young.

The family was poor, and Domenico could afford to give his children only a basic education. While they were still young, the children started working in their father's weaving business. The boys cleaned the wool, and their mother and sister spun the wool into yarn. Their father would then weave the wool into lengths of cloth.

Genova la Superba

When Christopher and his brothers and sister were growing up, Italy was not a united country, but was made up of a number of **city-states.** Genoa was an independent city-state ruled by a handful of powerful families. It was one of the most important and richest centers of trade in Europe, known as *Genova la Superba* (Genoa the Superb).

This engraving, from a 15th-century book called The Nuremberg Chronicles, *shows a view of the Italian port of Genoa. This is how the city would have looked when Columbus was young.*

The city's streets were lined with the marble palaces of **noble** families and rich merchants. The port was crowded with ships bringing silks and spices from the Far East, which were then sold to merchants from across Europe. The city was famous for its mapmakers, **navigators,** and shipbuilders. It also was famous for its bankers, who opened branches of their banks in all the main cities of Europe.

At the end of a tiring day in his father's workshop, Christopher would go down to the docks to watch the ships unload their valuable **cargoes.** He heard the sailors tell stories about faraway lands and must have longed to join them on journeys across the sea.

This 16th-century painting shows harvesters gathering peppercorns in the **Spice Islands,** which were major destinations for expeditions from Europe.

TRADE BARRIERS

In 1453, the Turks captured the ancient Greek city of Constantinople (now called Istanbul), gaining control of all the overland trade routes between Europe and the Far East. As a result, the silks and spices from the East that the Europeans loved so much became extremely expensive. The Italian ports of Genoa and Venice then became the main entry points for these goods into Europe. They grew very rich from the trade.

In a poet's words:

"So many are the Genoese
And so extended everywhere,
They go to any place they please
And re-create their city there."

(Taken from a poem written by an anonymous 15th-century poet of Genoa)

A New Life

Little is known about Columbus's youth, although he probably worked as a sailor from the age of about fourteen. In 1476, when he was 25, Columbus joined the crew of a merchant ship bound for northern Europe. However, they were attacked by another ship and sank 6 miles (9.5 kilometers) off Portugal. Columbus managed to swim ashore and traveled north to the capital city, Lisbon, where his brother Bartolomeo had already settled.

New skills and ideas

Lisbon was then the most important center of exploration in Europe. Bartolomeo was a successful mapmaker in the city, and Christopher probably joined him in his work. Determined to be an explorer, he taught himself mathematics, geography, and **astronomy.** He quickly earned a reputation as a skilled sailor and mapmaker.

In Columbus's words:

"During this time I have made it my business to read all that has been written on geography, history, philosophy, and other sciences."

(Taken from a letter written by Columbus in 1501 to the King and Queen of Spain)

Lisbon today is a thriving city. It was built on a number of hills overlooking the River Tagus, which leads directly to the Atlantic Ocean.

Dona Felipa

In about 1480, at age 29, Columbus married Felipa Perestrello e Moniz, the daughter of a Portuguese **noble** and governor of the island of Porto Santo, near Madeira. The young couple went to live on Porto Santo, and in 1481 Felipa gave birth to a son, Diego. Their marriage lasted only a short time—Felipa died, probably in 1483.

Columbus never married again, but he did have another son, Ferdinand (also called Fernando), with the woman he lived with for the rest of his life—Beatriz de Arana.

A new direction

While living on Porto Santo, Columbus made plans to sail to Japan by traveling westward across the Atlantic Ocean, then known as the "Ocean Sea." He thought he would be able to sail uninterrupted to the Far East, where he would find the silks, spices, and other luxuries so popular in Europe. Columbus's maps suggested that the journey would cover only 3,000 miles (4,800 kilometers), but the actual distance is more than 10,000 miles (16,000 kilometers)!

To organize the expedition, Columbus needed the support of King John II of Portugal. At the time, overland routes were closed to Europeans. In their quest for a sea route to the Far East, all Portuguese expeditions followed the west coast of Africa in search of a way east. Columbus believed his westward route would be quicker, but royal advisers thought this idea was eccentric. In 1485 the king refused to support Columbus, who then decided to try his luck in Spain.

D. JOÃO II

King John II of Portugal, who reigned from 1481 to 1495, sponsored many expeditions from Lisbon to the East.

Royal Support

In 1485, Columbus left Portugal with his five-year-old son Diego and crossed into southern Spain. Their first stop was the **monastery** of La Rábida near the small port of Palos de la Frontera. They were tired and hot, so Columbus asked the monks for food and water for his young son. Incredibly, stopping at the monastery started a chain of events that would change his life.

Influential contacts

While Columbus rested at La Rábida, he spoke to the **prior,** Juan Perez, who listened carefully to his plans and ideas for exploration. Perez introduced Columbus to another monk, Antonio de Marchena, who was not only a well-known **astronomer** but also had been **confessor** to Queen Isabella of Spain.

Leaving Diego behind at La Rábida to be educated by the monks, Columbus moved to the city of Seville. Using the monks' contacts, he was soon introduced to the Duke of Medina Celi, a rich Spanish **noble** and shipowner. The duke knew the king and queen and was sure they would be interested in Columbus's expedition plans.

This 19th-century painting shows Christopher Columbus and his son Diego arriving exhausted at the monastery of La Rábida. Their arrival there would eventually change the course of world history.

In 1486, Queen Isabella ordered Columbus to present his plans at the **royal court** in Cordoba. However, her main concern at this time was not exploration, but the **conquest** of the southern Spanish kingdom of Granada from its **Muslim** rulers. Although Columbus argued his case repeatedly, eventually, in 1490, the royal commissioners refused funding.

Getting ahead

In 1492, Granada fell to the Christian armies of Ferdinand and Isabella, and the queen was now able to turn her attention to Columbus's plans. She knew that the expeditions of Spain's great rival, Portugal, were getting closer and closer to the riches of India. It was vital that Spain find her own sea route to the East. Isabella gave Columbus her backing, and at long last the expedition that he had hoped for could begin.

In Columbus's words:

"Your Highnesses commanded me that, with a sufficient fleet, I should go to the said parts of India."

(Taken from *The Journal of Christopher Columbus*, written by his son Ferdinand)

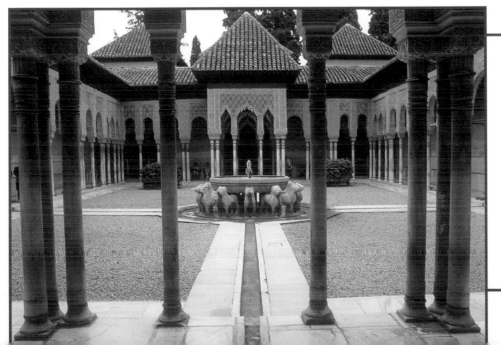

This is the Court of the Lions in the Alhambra palace. King Ferdinand and Queen Isabella took over this palace in Granada when they defeated the Muslim kingdom there in 1492.

Preparations for the Journey

Columbus, now 41 years old, felt that he would be too old to embark upon such an ambitious expedition if he waited much longer. Letters were sent from the king and queen of Spain, granting him all the ships and equipment he would need. They also promised to give him a tenth of all the "gold, silver, pearls, gems, spices, and other **merchandise**" he was expected to find. They would keep the rest.

Ships and crew

Columbus returned to the port of Palos as soon as he could, to begin preparations for the expedition. But royal advisers ordered the authorities in Palos to organize everything—three ships, crews, **ammunition,** and supplies—in just ten days, and to pay for two of the ships themselves. Such demands built great resentment in Palos against Columbus and his expedition. Many people also thought he was crazy to attempt to cross the Atlantic Ocean to reach the East.

> **In Columbus's words:**
>
> *"And I departed from the city of Granada on the twelfth day of the month of May in … 1492 … and came to the town of Palos, which is a port of the sea, where I made ready three ships …."*
>
> (Taken from *The Journal of Christopher Columbus*)

A map drawn in about 1490 shows the world as Columbus would have known it.

A helping hand

Some people, however, were prepared to support Columbus, including a number of bankers and merchants who were tempted by the promised riches. Another was a local shipowner, Martín Alonso Pinzón, who supplied two of the ships and recruited many sailors for the expedition. Some were criminals, released from prison, given a last chance to win fame and fortune.

The ships were loaded with supplies for the journey— barrels of water and beer, flour, rice, dried biscuits and beans, and even live chickens and pigs. Ropes and canvas were needed for repairs and guns to protect them from attack. After ten weeks of preparations, the ships were ready to sail.

*This statue of the Spanish **navigator** Martín Pinzón (1441–93) stands at Palos de la Frontera. He was regarded by many as the real hero of Columbus's expedition.*

PORTUGUESE RIVALS

In August 1487, King John II of Portugal sent out an expedition of three ships from Lisbon. It was led by Bartolomeu Dias (1450–1500), who had been instructed to find a sea route around Africa. Toward the end of 1487, the expedition sighted the southern tip of Africa. This was named the Cape of Good Hope, for a sea route to the riches of India and the East had been found. In 1497 Vasco da Gama reached India by sailing around the cape.

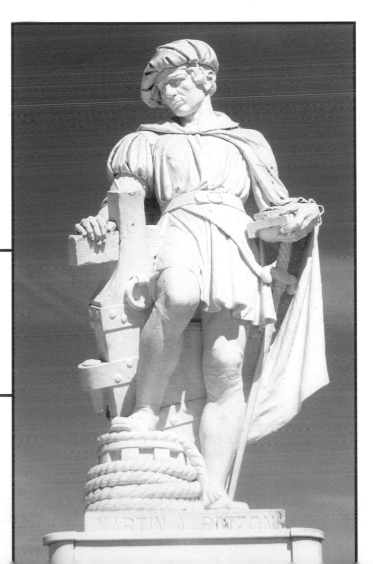

Life on Board

YOU CAN FOLLOW COLUMBUS'S FIRST EXPEDITION ON THE MAP ON PAGES 42–43.

At dawn on the morning of August 3, 1492, the three ships sailed quietly out of Palos to a sandbank called Saltes, where they waited for a wind to carry them westward. At 8:00 A.M. a gentle breeze blew up and filled the ships' sails, and they were soon on their way, heading southwest for the Canary Islands.

This engraving shows Columbus officially taking his leave from King Ferdinand and Queen Isabella. Isabella was the main driving force behind the Spanish expeditions.

Three small ships

Columbus's expedition consisted of three small ships, none longer than 79 feet (24 meters). Their names are now among the most famous in the history of exploration: the *Niña*, the *Pinta*, and the *Santa Maria*.

The *Santa Maria* was classed as a *nao*, a heavy **cargo** ship. She was the **flagship** of the expedition, and Columbus sailed on her as captain-general of the fleet. Also sailing on her were a number of royal officials, whose job was to take charge of the cargoes of exotic **merchandise** they hoped to bring back.

The *Niña* was really called the *Santa Clara*, but because she had once been owned by the Niño family of Palos, crew members called her *Niña*. The captain of the ship was Vincente, brother of Martín Pinzón. The *Niña* was a type of ship called a caravel, popular with Portuguese explorers. Its long, low, and narrow **hull** made it strong but nimble.

The *Pinta* was another caravel. She had three square sails, unlike the *Niña*, which had triangular "lateen" sails. Pinzón sailed on her as captain. His other brother, Francisco, was **master.**

This mId-17th century engraving depicts Columbus using navigational instruments.

Daily routine

Some of the officers, including Columbus, would have had their own cabins on board the ships, but everyone else would have slept on the lower decks on straw-filled sacks. Food was probably cooked on a **brazier** on the upper deck. There was little fresh food, and meals were usually porridge or soup made from grain, salted meat, and dry biscuits. Each day was divided into six "watches" of four hours each. A **lookout** always kept watch high up in the **crow's nest** on the ship's main mast.

Sailing Westward

YOU CAN FOLLOW COLUMBUS'S FIRST EXPEDITION ON THE MAP ON PAGES 42–43.

After years of planning and weeks of preparation, the expedition was finally on its way. Almost immediately after their departure from Spain, problems occurred. While many believed in Columbus's abilities, others did not. They still doubted the wisdom of the expedition.

Delayed in the Canaries

On the fourth day of the trip, the **rudder** on the *Pinta* broke. The fleet managed to limp into harbor in the Canary Islands, but it took a month before the damage was repaired. Columbus was certain that the owner of the *Pinta*, Cristobal Quintero, was plotting against him and had damaged it on purpose. Valuable time had been wasted, and the crews were growing impatient.

At last, at noon on September 6, the ships set sail again. Three days later they had completely lost sight of land and were entering unknown waters. The further they traveled out to sea, the more nervous the men became. Many feared they would never see their families again.

This is a view of the Canary Islands as they look today. Lying off the west coast of Africa, the group of islands was a vital stopping point for ships sailing from Europe on their way south and west.

The Santa Maria, *the* Niña, *and the* Pinta *sailed thousands of miles across unknown waters. Battered by winds and towering waves, they finally reached land more than two months later.*

First sighting

At about 10:00 P.M. on October 11, Columbus thought he could see a light flickering ahead of them "like a little wax candle rising and falling." He called out to two of his officers on the *Santa Maria*, but they could see nothing. At 2:00 A.M. the following morning, the **lookout** on the *Pinta* sighted land. A cannon was fired to announce the good news.

At dawn, the ships sailed into a bay and dropped anchor, 70 days after leaving Spain. On the beach, local people watched with amazement as Columbus and several officers rowed toward them. Columbus leapt out and dropped to his knees, giving thanks to God and claiming the land for the king and queen of Spain. The land they had reached was one of the islands now known as the Bahamas. The local people called it Guanahani, but Columbus renamed it San Salvador.

TWO DISTANCES

Columbus decided that two counts should be kept of the distance covered each day. One would be an accurate one for himself, while the other would give a reduced distance for the crew. He did this "in order that the men should not be discouraged or frightened by the excessive length of the journey." He also nailed a gold coin to the mast of the *Santa Maria*. It would be given to the first man who sighted land.

Exploration of the Indies

The people who lived on the island were the Taino. Columbus, however, was so convinced he had reached the **Indies** near India, and that beyond them must lie Japan and China, that he called the local people "Indians."

A tour of the islands

Columbus and his men were given a warm, but guarded, welcome by the Tainos. They exchanged food for some of the gifts the Spaniards had brought from Spain, such as small bells, knives, and glass beads. Potatoes and **cassava** plants were grown as food on the islands, and the people smoked the dry leaves of tobacco plants. All these were unknown to the Europeans.

> **In Columbus's words:**
>
> *"As soon as day broke, there came to the shore many of these men, all youths ... all of good height, very handsome people."*
>
> (From the log book of the *Santa Maria*, dated October 13, 1492)

After two days on San Salvador, Columbus sailed around the island to some of the neighboring islands, later reporting: "I saw so many islands that I could not decide to which I would go first." He gave each a new name. And everywhere he landed, he set up a Christian cross. On October 28, he reached Cuba, which he was certain must be Japan.

The lack of gold on San Salvador was a great disappointment to the Spaniards. But having learned a few words of the Taino language, they heard of an island where "the people gather gold on the beach by candles at night." This was enough to make Pinzón desert the expedition and take the *Pinta* in search of gold.

This woodcut illustration of 1493 shows Columbus touring the islands. The European artist has shown, on the left, a local ruler dressed as a European king.

This engraving shows Christopher Columbus on the island of Hispaniola, where he founded the first Spanish settlement in the Americas.

Home away from home

On December 6, 1192, Columbus reached the island that is now split between Haiti and the Dominican Republic. It reminded him so much of that Spain he named it Hispaniola. On Christmas Eve, as Columbus lay sleeping in his cabin, the *Santa Maria* ran aground on Hispaniola. The ship had to be abandoned, but Columbus saw in this disaster a sign from God. He named the site Puerto de la Navidad (Christmas Port) and left a group of 39 men there to build a fort from the boat **timbers.** The rest of the men transferred to the *Niña.*

YOU CAN FOLLOW COLUMBUS'S FIRST EXPEDITION ON THE MAP ON PAGES 42–43.

THE MEETING OF CULTURES

When Columbus first left Spain, Ferdinand and Isabella gave him strict instructions to treat any local people he might meet with respect. These good intentions did not last long. Within 50 years of Columbus's arrival, most of the local people on the islands had been killed through warfare, disease, and **persecution,** while others were sold into slavery.

The Return Journey

YOU CAN FOLLOW COLUMBUS'S FIRST EXPEDITION ON THE MAP ON PAGES 42–43.

On January 4, 1493, Columbus set sail on the *Niña,* bound for Spain. On board were six Taino men and a collection of birds, fruits, and plants, which were to be presented to King Ferdinand and Queen Isabella.

Across the ocean

As the *Niña* sailed away from Navidad, her crew spotted the *Pinta.* The two ships met, and Pinzón came aboard the *Niña.* According to Columbus, Pinzón gave him "invented excuses and false arguments" to explain his desertion. Although still very angry with Pinzón, Columbus preserved the peace.

The two ships sailed toward Spain together and were halfway back by February 9. However, they were soon caught in a great storm. It lasted for three whole days and nights. The two ships were tossed from side to side and eventually were separated from each other. When the storm died down the crew of each ship assumed the other had been lost, and so they continued their journeys back to Spain separately.

This late 15th-century illustration shows a sea creature off the coast of Hispaniola. Many sailors at this time believed that terrifying monsters lurked beneath the waves, waiting to devour them.

RIVALS

During the course of the expedition, Columbus and Pinzón grew very suspicious of each other. It was the **lookout** on Pinzón's ship, the *Pinta*, who had first spotted land, and Pinzón had deserted the expedition to look for gold. For years after Pinzón's death, his family and friends suggested that it was he, and not Columbus, who was really the hero of the expedition.

Quiet return

On March 4, 1493, the *Niña* sailed into the harbor at Lisbon. Columbus reported his findings to King John II of Portugal. Portugal and Spain were bitter rivals in trade and exploration. The Portuguese, particularly jealous of Columbus's success despite their having refused to support him in 1485, nearly had him murdered.

This view of Lisbon today is looking toward the harbor. The city has been an important port for centuries.

On March 15, Columbus and the *Niña* sailed back into the Spanish port of Palos. Pinzón, on the *Pinta*, had already reached northern Spain in February and had broken the news of the expedition's success. He arrived in Palos shortly after Columbus but fell gravely ill and died a few days later. With Pinzón dead, Columbus became the hero of the moment.

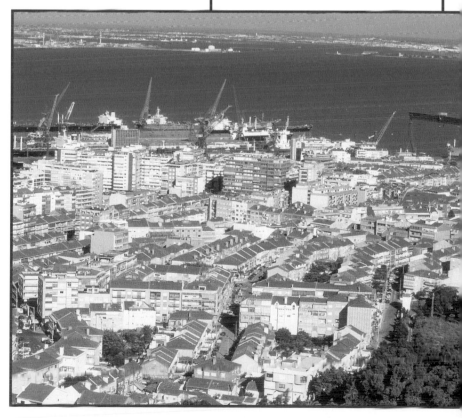

A Hero's Welcome

Columbus had been away seven months, and although he was very excited about his discoveries, he was also exhausted. So he rested for two weeks at the **monastery** of La Rábida and talked with **Prior** Perez, who had encouraged his exploration. He was also reunited with his sons Diego and Ferdinand, who had been cared for in nearby Seville.

Royal reception

Ferdinand and Isabella summoned Columbus to their **royal court,** located in Barcelona in northeastern Spain, to speak of his journey. He had to travel a long way from the south to the north of Spain, so he organized a spectacular procession to publicize his great achievement.

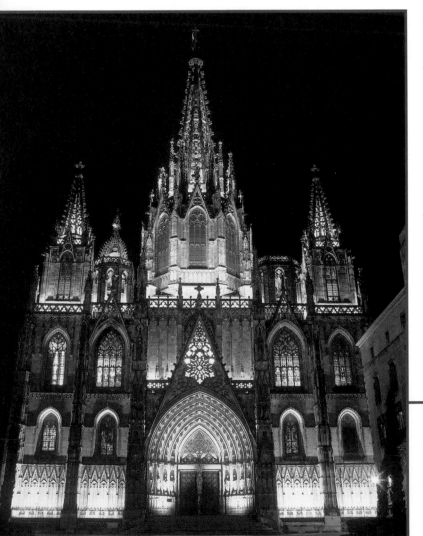

At the front of the procession were the six Taino dressed in gold ornaments, followed by souvenirs such as colorful parrots in fancy cages and exotic plants. Columbus rode on horseback at the end, waving to the hundreds of cheering people along the route.

This is Barcelona Cathedral, where a celebration mass was said to mark Columbus's return.

When they finally reached Barcelona, "all the court and city came out." Columbus was ushered into the audience chamber, where he knelt before the king and queen. They ordered him to rise and sit in a place of honor beside the queen. He told them all about the expedition and the adventures along the way, while the Taino and souvenirs were shown off.

Following Columbus's triumphant presentation at the royal court at Barcelona, the six Taino stayed with him throughout his time in Spain. Five of them returned to their island on Columbus's second expedition, while one remained behind at the Spanish royal court, where he died two years later.

Golden promises

Everyone in Barcelona was sure that Columbus had found a new route to the **Indies.** Columbus pointed to the gold ornaments worn by the Taino and said that much more would be found. Impressed by these promises of great future riches, royal approval was given to a second expedition, and Columbus was appointed "Governor of the islands that he has discovered in the Indies."

This gold Spanish coin shows the heads of Ferdinand and Isabella. Columbus would have taken coins such as this on his voyages.

In Columbus's words:

"In conclusion, … their Highnesses can see that I will give them as much gold as they may need, if their Highnesses will render me very slight assistance; presently, I will give them spices and cotton, as much as their Highnesses shall command …."

(Written by Columbus on February 15, 1493, in a letter describing the results of his first voyage)

Columbus's Second Expedition

Although he had no real proof of it, Columbus's tales of abundant gold on the islands bewitched many of his listeners. Hundreds of young men begged him to take them on his next voyage. Unlike his first expedition, this time he had no difficulty in recruiting volunteers.

The King and Queen appointed Don Juan de Fonseca, Archdeacon of Seville, to the new position of Superintendent of the Affairs of the **Indies.** It was his job to organize all the preparations for the second expedition. In a few months, he managed to equip 17 ships with enough supplies to last 6 months and recruited 1,200 sailors. Among them was Columbus's younger brother Diego.

*Shown here is Guadaloupe **monastery,** where Columbus stayed after the celebrations for his return to Spain.*

This is Pope Alexander VI, painted in about 1506 by the famous Italian artist Titian. With the Treaty of Tordesillas in 1494, the Pope divided the known world between Spain and Portugal.

The official instructions for the second expedition were dated May 29, 1493. They stated that the main purpose of the expedition was to **convert** the local people to Christianity. Columbus had described them as **"idolators."** Ferdinand and Isabella strongly believed it was their royal duty to convert all the people who lived in the lands ruled by them to the **Catholic** religion. Among the travelers were Father Bernado Buil, **chaplain** to the fleet, and four other priests.

The second important objective was to establish a trading colony. Columbus also was instructed to make detailed maps of all the islands. A third and perhaps most important objective was to find gold.

Builders and farmers were also recruited and brought seeds, plants, and farm animals with them. This was to be a full-scale expedition of **colonization.** Most of the men came from the southern Spanish region of Andalusia and some had been on Columbus's first voyage. Soldiers, cavalrymen, and their horses were also on board, for this was to be an expedition of **conquest** as well as of trade.

WORDS OF DOUBT

While most people were willing to believe that Columbus really had found a sea route to the riches of the East, some were not so sure. One of them, an Italian living in Spain named Pietro Martire d'Anghiera, studied Columbus's accounts of his first journey. From these he concluded that it was highly unlikely that Columbus had gone as far as Asia. D'Anghiera believed Columbus had found a "New World" unknown to Europeans, but he did not realize the islands fringed an entirely new continent.

A Gloomy Return

On September 25, 1493, the fleet of ships set sail from the southern Spanish port of Cádiz. Their first stop was the Canary Islands, where they took on board more food and other supplies.

These are the docks at the port of Cádiz in southern Spain. Cádiz is one of the oldest cities in Spain, and its port has been one of the busiest and most important for thousands of years.

A quick crossing

On his second expedition, Columbus chose a more southerly route. The ships battled through one storm along the way, but most of the journey was smooth and quick. On Sunday, November 3, just 22 days after leaving the Canaries, the **lookouts** sighted an island to the south of Hispaniola. Columbus named it Dominica, which is the Spanish word for "Sunday."

Columbus explored other islands around Dominica. He named one of these Guadeloupe after the famous **monastery** in Spain. As the ships lay offshore, one of his captains, Diego Marquez, disobeyed orders and went ashore. He quickly got lost in the thick forests that covered the island, and search parties were sent to find him.

YOU CAN FOLLOW COLUMBUS'S SECOND EXPEDITION ON THE MAP ON PAGES 42–43.

Telling tales

As the men hacked their way through the **vegetation,** they saw many beautiful trees and sweet-smelling plants that were unknown in Europe. On their return to the ships, they also claimed to have seen some terrifying sights on the island. Guadeloupe was populated by the fierce Carib people, who were greatly feared by the more peaceful Taino and Arawak of the other islands. The Spanish sailors returned to their ships with stories of human limbs hanging from trees and captured young Taino children being fattened up for cooking.

Marquez was eventually found and the ships sailed on. The expedition reached the eastern coast of Hispaniola on November 22 and five days later landed at Navidad. Far from being greeted by the settlers, they were met by an eerie silence and the sight of the blackened ruins of the wooden fort. They learned from local Taino that all the settlers had been **massacred** by a raiding party of Arawak from the center of the island.

Many of the plants, fruits, and vegetables that Columbus and his men found on the islands, such as tobacco, pineapples, and potatoes, were exported back to Spain. They eventually had a great effect on European society. The pineapple was highly prized by kings, while the potato changed the farming economies of Europe forever.

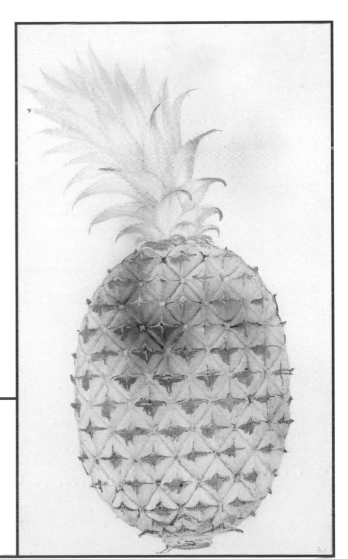

Shown here is a late 16th-century illustration of a pineapple. Following the European discovery of the Americas, many new fruits, vegetables, and other plants were taken back to Europe.

Success Turns to Disaster

This woodcut illustration shows the destruction of the Spanish settlement of Navidad. Columbus was told that the Chief Caonabo of the Arawak attacked and burned the settlement.

You can follow Columbus's second expedition on the map on pages 42–43.

Columbus was horrified to see the ruins of Navidad, but he refused to be discouraged. He ordered the fleet to sail on around Hispaniola in search of a new site for a settlement, near where Columbus believed they would find gold.

A new settlement

The journey around Hispaniola was extremely difficult. They were sailing against screaming winds and strong currents. After 25 days they had managed to cover only 30 miles (48 kilometers). Eventually, on January 2, 1494, they found a bay where they could build shelter. Columbus sent men ashore to start building a new settlement. He named it Isabella, in honor of the queen who had given him so much support in "the enterprise of the **Indies.**"

Columbus and a small force of armed men explored the interior of Hispaniola. They crossed a range of mountains and saw a vast, beautiful plain stretching out before them, which Columbus named Vega Real, or Royal Plain. When he returned to Isabella, the settlement was in chaos. The men complained the site was unhealthy, as many had fallen ill. They also complained that they had been tricked into joining the expedition. Where was the gold Columbus had promised?

Fighting to survive

To prevent a **mutiny,** Columbus had the main troublemakers arrested. Leaving his brother Diego in charge of the settlement, he left to explore Cuba, which he still believed was Japan. On his return to Isabella, Columbus found that his brother Bartolomeo had arrived from Spain with fresh supplies. His joy at the reunion was short-lived—a large group of Arawak had gathered on the Vega Real to attack the settlement. Columbus led a small army out from the settlement and destroyed the invaders.

This victory could not hide the fact that the expedition was in shambles. News of the problems had reached the ears of Ferdinand and Isabella in Spain, who were becoming very concerned. Columbus decided he had to return to Spain in order to clear his name.

The Battle of Vega Real in 1494 was the first real confrontation between the Spanish **colonists** and the local people. Columbus led a small force of 200 foot soldiers, 20 cavalry, and 20 hunting dogs against several thousand Arawak warriors. This was the first time the local people had seen horses and guns.

In Columbus's words:

"Evil words arose in Spain and belittlement of the enterprise which had been begun there, because I had not at once dispatched ships laden with gold ...."

(From a letter written by Columbus in his own defense to the King and Queen of Spain)

This engraving of 1594 by Theodore de Bry shows a rebellion of Native Americans against Spanish settlers. At the Battle of Vega Real, local people tried to drive the Spaniards off their land.

The Third Expedition

YOU CAN FOLLOW COLUMBUS'S THIRD EXPEDITION ON THE MAP ON PAGES 42–43.

Columbus left Hispaniola for Spain with two ships on March 10, 1496. For more than two years he had struggled with all sorts of problems on the island. One of his main failures, in the eyes of his Spanish backers, was that he had so far found very little gold or **merchandise** to take back to Spain.

In defense

Columbus arrived in Cádiz on June 11, 1496, to a quiet reception. He hurried north to meet the king and queen in the city of Burgos. A royal investigation had already cleared Columbus of any wrongdoing on the expedition. Ferdinand and Isabella also chose not to believe the stories that were being told against him. They had enough confidence in Columbus to give their approval to a third expedition. However, others plotted against him, and it took two years before his new expedition was ready to sail.

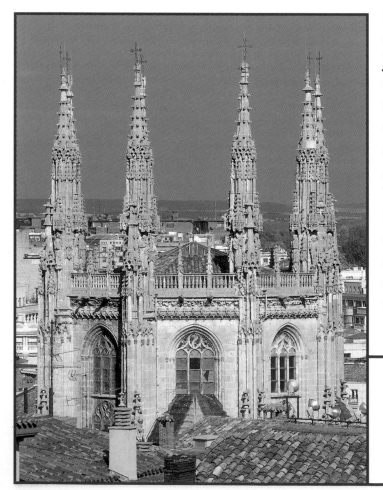

Eight ships sailed in the third expedition. Two ships left in January of 1498 and sailed directly to Hispaniola. The other six left four months later from the Canaries. Three of these sailed to the Cape Verde Islands, off the west coast of Africa. Traveling south towards the Equator, the ships entered the **doldrums.** With no winds or currents to carry them along, they lay stranded for eight days under the blazing sun.

This is Burgos Cathedral in northern Spain, where the King and Queen would spend the hot summer months in the cooler cities to the north of the country.

At last a small breeze carried them further westward. On July 31, three mountain peaks were spotted in the distance. Columbus named them Trinidad. The ships sailed on to the Gulf of Paria and along a shoreline, which Columbus thought must be that of another island. In fact, they were sailing along the coast of South America, near present-day Venezuela.

Clapped in irons

While Columbus had been in Spain, his brothers Diego and Bartolomeo had abandoned the unhealthy site at Isabella. They founded a new settlement, which they named Santo Domingo. When Columbus arrived at Santo Domingo, he found the settlers fighting among themselves. He again tried to impose law and order, and several settlers were **executed.**

Alarmed at this latest twist of events, Ferdinand and Isabella sent a royal official, Francisco de Bobadilla, to investigate. Upon reaching Santo Domingo in August of 1500, he found the settlers still fighting. He had Columbus and his brothers arrested and shipped back to Spain in chains.

> ### In Columbus's words:
>
> *"Here by God's will I have brought under the dominion of our Sovereigns a new world ... I should be judged as a captain .... No pirate treated a merchant like this!"*
>
> (From a letter written by Columbus while under arrest)

This illustration shows Columbus and his ships arriving at Trinidad, with an inset portrait of Columbus on the left.

In Disgrace

"There go the sons of the Admiral of Mosquitoes, of the man who discovered the lands of vanity and fraud, the cemetery of Castilian **noblemen.**" People of Seville shouted out insults such as this to Columbus's two sons, Diego and Ferdinand. They were being brought up at the Spanish **royal court** in Seville, because their father was being returned to Spain a prisoner.

Christopher Columbus refused to have his chains removed until he was brought before King Ferdinand and Queen Isabella of Spain. He always kept his chains and even wanted to be buried in them when he died.

In Columbus's words:

"... in disgrace, low in the favor of these monarchs, and with little money."

(Columbus's own description of his situation at this time)

Fallen angels

The ship reached Cádiz in November of 1500, but six weeks passed before Columbus received a royal summons to meet the king and queen. When he entered their **audience chamber** in Granada, Columbus bowed low before Ferdinand and Isabella. They responded with the same kindness and respect as before, and his chains were removed.

Ferdinand and Isabella reassured him that he would be restored as **governor** of the **Indies.** But after many months, he heard that he was to be replaced by Nicolás de Ovando, who set sail from Spain in February of 1502 with a fleet of 30 ships and 2,500 men.

One last chance

However, the king and queen gave Columbus permission to lead a fourth expedition to find a westward passage to India, China, and the **Spice Islands.** He set sail from Cádiz in four ships on May 9, 1502, this time accompanied by his second son Ferdinand, who was twelve years old.

VASCO DA GAMA (C.1460–1524)

In July of 1497, as Columbus was still trying to find a westward route to India, a fleet of 4 ships and 170 men set sail south from Lisbon in Portugal. It was led by a Portuguese nobleman named Vasco da Gama. After ten months at sea, the fleet finally reached Calicut on the west coast of India. The Portuguese had won the race to the Indies.

*The Portuguese explorer Vasco da Gama was the first European to sail around the coast of Africa to India. The discovery of this route started **colonization** of the Far East by Europeans.*

JOHN CABOT (C.1450–C.1498)

After Columbus's supposed achievement in reaching the "Indies," King Henry VII of England gave support to another Italian, Giovanni Caboto (John Cabot), to sail across the Atlantic. In 1497, he reached the coast of Canada, which he believed to be Asia. He embarked on another expedition in 1498 but never returned.

Endless Wanderings

You can follow Columbus's fourth expedition on the map on pages 42–43.

Columbus was 51 years old when he set out on his fourth expedition. He was in a great deal of pain, suffering from **arthritis** and poor eyesight. Although he had been treated kindly by Ferdinand and Isabella, he still felt humiliated and angry that he had been replaced as **governor.**

An unwelcome visitor

On June 29, 1502, Columbus and his small fleet reached the new settlement of Santo Domingo. He had been refused permission by Ferdinand and Isabella to land there, because they were afraid he would pick a fight with the new governor, Nicolás de Ovando. He continued westward to find a passage to India. By the end of July he had reached the coast of Central America, where he exchanged goods with the local people.

THE DEATH OF BOBADILLA

At Santo Domingo, Columbus sent a message warning that a violent storm was heading for Hispaniola. However, ignoring this warning, about 26 ships still left for Spain. All but one were destroyed in the storm and their crews drowned. Among these lost men was Juan de Bobadilla, Columbus's former jailer and sworn enemy. The single ship to survive was one carrying Columbus's possessions.

Between mid-August and mid-September, as they were sailing along the coast of the country now known as Honduras, Columbus's fleet ran into violent storms. Columbus recorded in his log book that "the ships lay exposed to the weather, with sails torn and anchors, rigging, cables, boats, and many of the stores lost" for 28 days.

This aerial photograph of the coast of Honduras was taken in 1998, soon after Hurricane Mitch had blown across the land. Columbus had to battle against terrible storms off the coast of Honduras.

Veragua

Columbus's fleet spent months sailing back and forth along the coastline of Central America, trying in vain to reach the **Indies.** On about January 6, 1503, unable to go any further, the ships dropped anchor at the mouth of a river and the men rowed ashore. The local people called this land Veragua. Today it is known as Panama.

With few supplies and fearing attack by local warriors, the fleet headed south to Santo Domingo. Two ships were leaking so badly they had to be abandoned. The men crowded onto the remaining two ships. As they sank lower and lower into the water, it became clear that these ships were not going to last the journey. Finally, on June 25, the ships ran aground on Jamaica.

This illustration shows Columbus landing at Veragua (Panama), with a portrait of his brother Bartolomeo on the right.

Mutiny and Rescue

Columbus and his men were stranded on Jamaica. The two ships were unfit to sail again, but the crew built straw-roofed huts on the decks for shelter.

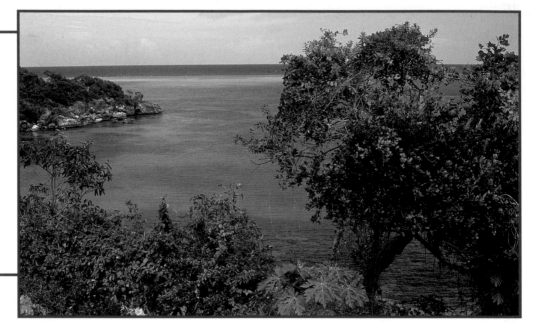

This is a photograph of the coast of Jamaica today. Columbus and his crew were shipwrecked in similar surroundings for a whole year.

A long wait

Columbus hoped it would not be too long before they were rescued. However, no gold had been found on Jamaica, and very few ships passed in their direction. In the end, they were stranded a whole year on Jamaica.

When the last of the food had been eaten, a young officer named Diego Mendez took three sailors and journeyed inland. Some local Taino people they met exchanged fresh food for Spanish goods, but others grew restless at the Spaniards' presence.

A TERRIBLE WARNING

When the Taino refused to supply them with any more food, Columbus devised a trick. Knowing that an **eclipse** of the moon would take place on the next night, he warned the Taino that this would be a sign of God's anger. When the moon disappeared from sight as predicted, the terrified Taino begged Columbus to restore it to the skies and agreed to renew their supplies of food.

A great gamble

Realizing that the expedition was in great danger, Columbus persuaded Mendez and another officer to paddle a Taino canoe across the sea to Hispaniola, 100 miles (161 kilometers) away, to get help. Few of those left behind expected them to survive such a dangerous journey.

As time went on, some rebel Spaniards began to believe Columbus had stranded them deliberately. One day a group of them attacked Columbus and his loyal followers, shouting, "Kill the Admiral and his men!" In the battle that followed, some of the rebels were killed and the rest were forced to move to another part of the island.

After four days of rowing, Mendez managed to reach Hispaniola and raise the alarm. However, **governor** Ovando was in no hurry to rescue the troublesome Columbus. Eventually, on June 28, 1504, a ship reached Jamaica to take the bedraggled men back to Santo Domingo. When Columbus, tired and sick, stepped ashore two weeks later, Ovando greeted him. Columbus's son Ferdinand described this false show of affection as "the kiss of a scorpion."

YOU CAN FOLLOW COLUMBUS'S FOURTH EXPEDITION ON THE MAP ON PAGES 42–43.

In Columbus's words:

"Let me only say, my Lord, that my hope has been and is that you will not spare yourself to save me, and I am certain of it, for all my senses inform me."

(From a letter written by Columbus to Ovando and sent with Mendez)

This is the coat of arms granted to Christopher Columbus and his descendants. At the top is the castle of Castile and the lion of León in Spain. At the bottom are the islands Columbus discovered and the ships' anchors, representing his naval background.

The End of an Extraordinary Life

A month after being rescued, at the end of July 1504, Columbus and most of his men set sail homeward for Spain. He was now 53 years old and white-haired. He would never again return to the islands that he had first reached twelve years earlier.

A forgotten voice

After a rough crossing, the ship eventually reached the port of Sanlucar de Barrameda, near Seville, on November 7. Columbus was now a very sick man and was convinced that he had only a few more years to live. In his remaining years, he was determined to fight to restore his good name and to win back the fortune he felt he had been cheated out of when replaced as **governor.**

Columbus's hopes were dashed when Queen Isabella died just nine days after he returned. He wrote letters to Ferdinand, hoping for royal support, but had no response. He was increasingly ignored as the rush to **colonize** and profit from the New World gathered speed.

DEATH OF QUEEN ISABELLA

On November 26, 1504, Queen Isabella died in the city of Medina del Campo. She was 53 years old, the same age as Columbus. Her body was taken back for burial in her tomb in the cathedral of Granada, where it rests today. With her death, Columbus lost his most loyal and powerful patron.

Final days

Columbus was too ill to travel from Seville to meet the king himself. His son Diego was now attached to the **royal court** and handled his father's affairs. Columbus eventually managed to travel to Segovia, where he met the King. Ferdinand listened to him politely, but Columbus's pleas were ignored. On May 20, 1506, Christopher Columbus died in a Franciscan **monastery** in the city of Valladolid, with his two sons, Diego and Ferdinand, and his brother Diego by his bed.

Even after his death, however, Christopher Columbus never stopped traveling. His body was first buried in the monastery in Valladolid, but three years later his son Diego had it transferred to a new family tomb in Seville. After Diego's own death, Columbus's bones were taken all the way to Santo Domingo. In 1795, when Hispaniola was captured by the French, the bones were moved to Havana in Cuba. Finally, in 1898, they were returned to Spain and buried in an elaborate tomb in the cathedral of Seville. There they remain to this day.

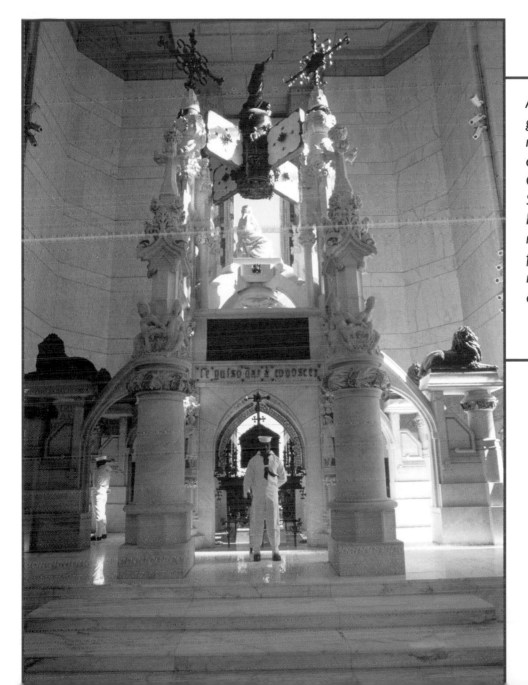

A sailor stands guard at the magnificent tomb of Christopher Columbus in Seville Cathedral. His body was moved to this final resting place nearly 400 years after his death.

Columbus's Legacy

You can follow the routes of Columbus's four expeditions on pages 42–43.

Christopher Columbus is famous throughout the world as the explorer who "discovered" America. However, he died still believing that he had reached the **Indies** and that Japan and China lay just beyond.

If he had explored the coastlines of Central and South America more during his third and fourth expeditions, Columbus might have realized that he had found an entire continent. However, it was another Italian explorer, Amerigo Vespucci (1451–1512), who first described the continent in a book published in 1507, the year after Columbus's death. It was thus named "America" after him rather than "Columbia" after Columbus.

THE VIKINGS IN AMERICA

We now know that Columbus was not the first European to reach the Americas. That was achieved in about 1000, when a party of Vikings led by Leif Eriksson landed on the northeastern coast of America, where Newfoundland is today. They made a number of settlements but all ended in failure, and the route west from Europe was forgotten until Columbus made the journey 500 years later.

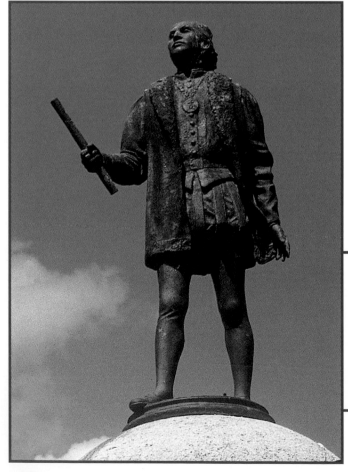

This statue of Christopher Columbus stands at St. Anne's Bay, Jamaica. After Columbus first sailed to the area, many more European explorers followed and colonized the Caribbean islands and the mainland of America.

Changing history

No other journey of exploration has led to as much as Columbus's journeys have. His discoveries, and those of explorers who came after him, opened the way to the European **colonization** of America. This ultimately created great wealth in Spain and the rest of Europe, but it also led to the complete destruction of many ancient ways of life.

Through **persecution** and ignorance, a new culture, religion, and language were imposed upon the local people. Today, many Native American people feel very bitter that for centuries their traditional customs and religions were crushed and swept aside. They are now trying to revive many of their old traditions.

Magnificent failure

Columbus boasted, bullied, exaggerated, and lied. Most of his expeditions ended in failure and even disaster, and he died a broken and bitter man. Even so, his achievement was incredible. His unwavering belief in himself and his missions led him to survive shipwreck, rebellion, and disease. He has been described as a magnificent failure, but his failure to find a way to the Indies led to an even greater success: the rediscovery of America for Europe. By achieving this, Columbus changed the course of history forever.

This map of the New World, made in 1608 by the Dutch mapmaker Pieter Van Den Keere, is based upon Columbus's voyage of 1492 and shows many of the islands he discovered.

Map of Columbus's Expeditions

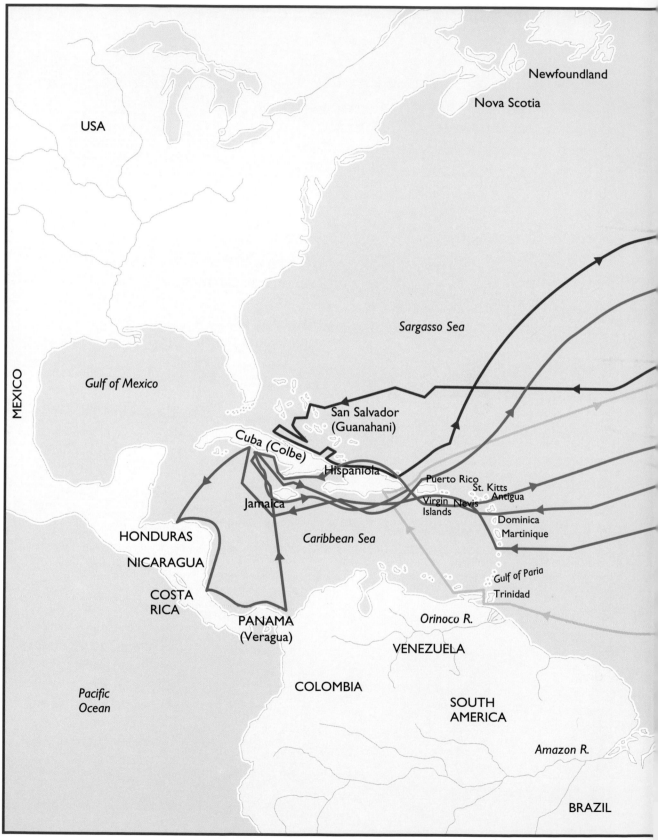

Newfoundland

Nova Scotia

USA

Sargasso Sea

MEXICO

Gulf of Mexico

San Salvador
(Guanahani)

Cuba (Colbe)

Hispaniola

Puerto Rico

St. Kitts
Antigua

Virgin Nevis
Islands

Dominica

Martinique

Jamaica

Caribbean Sea

HONDURAS

NICARAGUA

Gulf of Paria

Trinidad

COSTA
RICA

PANAMA
(Veragua)

Orinoco R.

VENEZUELA

Pacific
Ocean

COLOMBIA

SOUTH
AMERICA

Amazon R.

BRAZIL

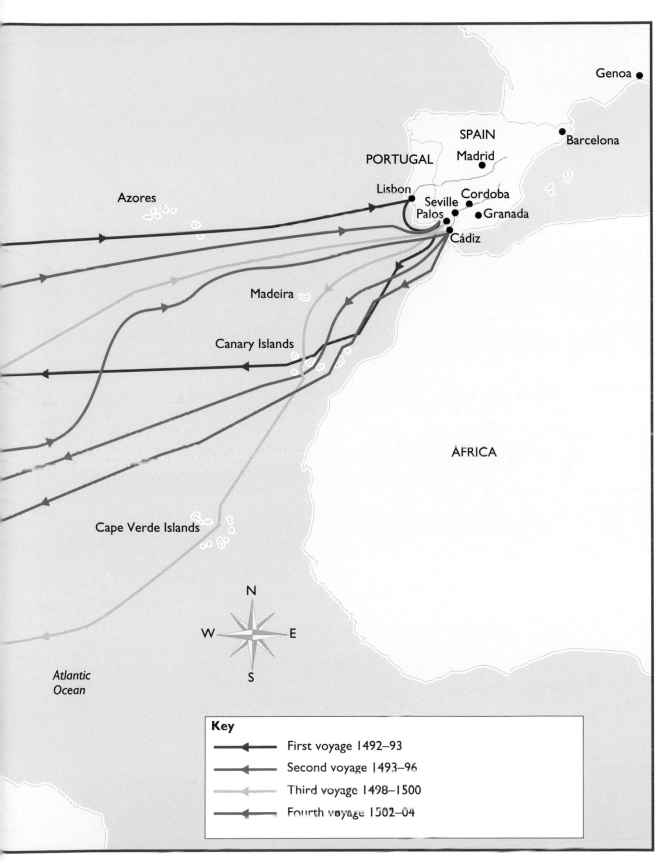

Genoa

SPAIN

Barcelona

PORTUGAL

Madrid

Lisbon

Azores

Seville   Cordoba
Palos

Granada

Cádiz

Madeira

Canary Islands

AFRICA

Cape Verde Islands

N

W   E

S

Atlantic
Ocean

Key

First voyage 1492–93

Second voyage 1493–96

Third voyage 1498–1500

Fourth voyage 1502–04

Timeline

1451	Christopher Columbus is born in Genoa, Italy.
1453	The Turks capture Constantinople (now called Istanbul), the capital city of the Byzantine Empire.
1469	King Ferdinand of Aragon and Queen Isabella of Castile are married.
1476	Columbus moves to Lisbon, Portugal.
1480	Columbus marries Felipa Perestrello e Moniz.
1481	Diego Columbus is born.
1483	Felipa Perestrello e Moniz dies.
1485	Columbus moves to Spain after King John II of Portugal refuses to support his expedition.
1486	Queen Isabella summons Columbus to the **royal court.**
1487	A Portuguese expedition under the command of Bartolemeu Dias sails as far as the southern tip of Africa.
1490	The rulers of Spain refuse to fund Columbus's expedition.
1492	Ferdinand and Isabella capture the southern Spanish city of Granada and agree to support Columbus. His first expedition sets sail for the East on August 3 and arrives in North America on October 12.
1493	Columbus returns in triumph to Spain.
	Columbus's second expedition sets sail.
1494	The battle of Vega Real takes place.
1496	Columbus returns to Spain.
1497	John Cabot, sailing from England, reaches the coast of Canada.

1498	Columbus's third expedition sets sail.
	A Portuguese expedition under Vasco da Gama reaches the port of Calicut in India.
1500	Columbus is arrested and shipped back to Spain.
1502	Nicolás de Ovando is appointed new **governor** of the **Indies.**
	Columbus sets sail on his fourth and final expedition.
1503	Columbus is shipwrecked on Jamaica.
1504	Columbus returns to Spain for the last time.
	Queen Isabella of Spain dies.
1506	Columbus dies.
1507	America is named after Amerigo Vespucci.
1961	The remains of a Viking settlement are found at L'Anse aux Meadows, Canada, proving that Columbus was not the first European in North America.
1971	Columbus Day becomes a national holiday in the United States. It is celebrated on October 12.

More Books to Read

Gallagher, Carole. *Christopher Columbus and the Discovery of the New World.* Broomall, Penn.: Chelsea House Publishers, 2000.

Isaacs, Sally Senzell. *America in the Time of Columbus: From Earliest Times to 1590.* Chicago, Ill.: Heinemann Library, 1998.

Roop, Peter and Connie. *Christopher Columbus.* New York: Scholastic, 2001.

Glossary

ammunition missiles, such as bullets or rockets, that are shot from a weapon such as a gun or cannon

arthritis inflammation of the joints that can cause severe pain and stiffness

astronomy study of the stars and planets

audience chamber official room where a ruler or head of state receives visitors

brazier metal basket for burning charcoal

cargo goods carried on board a ship

cassava type of plant, native to the New World, with roots that can be used as food

chaplain priest or minister who is officially attached to a branch of the military, a court, or an expedition

city-state independent state made up of a single city and its surrounding territories

colonization act of settling a land with new people

confessor a priest who acts as someone's regular spiritual guide

conquer to gain control of a place or people. Such an act is called "conquest."

convert to change someone's religious beliefs by persuasion, either by choice or by force

crow's nest lookout platform high up on a ship's mast

doldrums area of the sea along the Equator where there is very little wind

eclipse total or partial covering of the Sun or Moon. A lunar eclipse occurs when Earth passes between the Sun and the Moon.

execute to put a person to death

flagship most important ship in a fleet, on which the commander of the fleet travels

governor person who governs or rules a province on behalf of a monarch or other head of state

hull main body of a ship

Indies islands once believed to lie off India, Japan, and China

idolator someone who worships "idols," or statues of gods

lookout person on board a ship who is appointed to keep watch against danger

massacre to kill brutally in large numbers

master person who is licensed to command a merchant ship

merchandise goods bought and sold by merchants and shopkeepers

monastery residence of a religious community of monks

Muslim follower of the religion of Islam

mutiny rebellion by sailors against their senior officers

navigator person in charge of plotting a route and directing a ship along it

noble person of high birth or rank

persecution ill-treatment of people because of their culture, religion, or appearance

prior head of a religious community

royal court official household of a king or queen

rudder large steering paddle at the stern (back) of a ship

Spice Islands islands in Southeast Asia, now known as the Molucca or Maluku Islands of Indonesia, where many spices are grown

timbers shaped wooden pieces used to build a ship

vegetation group of different plants growing in a place

Index